This Is The Love You Deserve

THOUGHT CATALOG BOOKS

This Is The Love You Deserve

THOUGHT CATALOG

THOUGHT CATALOG BOOKS

Brooklyn, NY

THOUGHT CATALOG BOOKS

Copyright © 2016 by The Thought & Expression Co.

All rights reserved. Published by Thought Catalog Books, a division of The Thought & Expression Co., Williamsburg, Brooklyn. Founded in 2010, Thought Catalog is a website and imprint dedicated to your ideas and stories. We publish fiction and non-fiction from emerging and established writers across all genres. For general information and submissions: manuscripts@thoughtcatalog.com.

First edition, 2016

ISBN 978-1535025577

10 9 8 7 6 5 4 3 2 1

Cover photography by © Greg Rakozy

Contents

1

For The Hearts That Are No Longer Broken

Rose Stein

Wow. Look at you! Look how far you have come. There was a time where you didn't think you would mend. You believed you would stay broken. You didn't think you would heal. But here you are. You are so happy, you are so full. It is as if you are brand new. A stronger, more vibrant, and complete version of yourself.

You didn't believe me at first when I told you time heals everything. You didn't think you were strong. You doubted yourself. You thought you would never love again. You thought you would be stuck in that place. A place of darkness, of hurt, of sadness.

I'm glad you decided to listen to me. You opened yourself to love; you opened yourself to a new chapter. There are so many things that you have accomplished because of this. You chose love over fear. Though one love was lost, you knew you would love again. **This time, you chose to love yourself. The most important love of all.**

There was a time where you felt lost, broken, defeated. You

felt yourself slipping, but you decided to pick yourself back up. You gathered the pieces of yourself that were scattered across the floor, stood up, dusted off your clothes, and started to walk forward.

You no longer look back but are grateful for everything that came before you. Though the future is still uncertain, you do not allow fear to control you. You know that everything happened for a reason, and your journey is just as important as your destination. You are happy to be right where you are, right in this very moment. You are no longer lost, because you have found yourself.

I am so proud of you! For everything you have accomplished. For finding light, even in a dark place. For allowing yourself to let go. For allowing yourself to heal. For opening yourself to new opportunities, to the universe, and to love. Everything you have gone through, led you to where you are now.

And, where you are now, is exactly where you are meant to be.

2

You Have To Fall Back In Love With Yourself To Move On From A Breakup

Beau Taplin

Here you are again, with your head cradled in your hands and your heart pounding like a wrecking ball against the walls of your chest. Maybe you left, or maybe they did, it doesn't matter—the fact is you're in treacherous territory, minus a best friend, and wondering which way is the right way forward. The first and most important thing to remember about letting go is it is one of the only things in the world that doesn't get easier with experience or practice, because it's different every time. Every connection you develop with another human being is unique to itself and requires its own strategy to sever, but there are a few general guidelines you can follow.

Avoid quick fixes at all costs. The solution to a broken heart isn't finding something else to seal the wound, but falling back in love with your solitary self; it is relearning how to enjoy the company of your thoughts, and trust in your instincts and ability to navigate a life on your own. Though a rebound may well be gratifying in the moment, it will keep you dependent on others for happiness, and before long you'll find yourself leaping from one thing to another until love is no longer love at all, but a stepping stone, a way safely through to the other side without ever being required to face a thing alone. You deserve so much more than that.

And here's why: If others find you unique and desirable and enjoyable to be around, why shouldn't you feel that way about yourself? Why shouldn't you take time to appreciate your own company and get back in touch with your own desires and hopes? After some soul-searching you may find that you have gone off track, that somewhere along the way you have lost sight of what really matters and now you have an opportunity to find your way back. Take advantage of that.

I believe wholeheartedly that every plight and predicament in life has a purpose, one that if harnessed sensibly can be used to help you grow and better yourself as a human being. Breakups are no different. Rather than wallow in self-pity and sadness, choose instead to rise above it, to take the challenge, reassess your wishes and wants, and rediscover yourself. Believe me, you might just like what you find.

3

10 Signs You're On The Verge Of Finding Real Love

Brianna Wiest

1. You've finally realized that romantic love is not the end-all-be-all of your existence.

It is no longer your top priority, most unrelenting obsession, or deepest interest. You are not solely invested in finding someone else to give you the attention and respect and admiration you now know how to give yourself.

2. You're starting to focus on the love you can give, not the love you can get.

You want to love someone as much as you want to be loved; you're going into your relationships with the mindset of "What can I offer?" as opposed to "What can I get?"

3. You've taken enough time to work on yourself.

You don't have to be perfect to be loved, but for a relationship to work, if not thrive, you need to have any real crippling emotional issues at least addressed beforehand.

4. You're hurt, not devastated, over your last breakup.

If you didn't mourn the loss of someone in your life you wouldn't be sane, but when it gets to the point of utter devastation, it's usually a signal that you were unhealthily attached, not actually in love.

5. You want a relationship, but not desperately so.

Yes, you want to date, and yes, you do want to maybe find someone you can commit to, but you aren't broken or reeling if this isn't the case. You still have a life to run outside of your romantic interests.

6. You've let go of the idea that you can predict, or measure, whether or not someone is "right" for you.

You've tossed the "checklist" out the window and are starting to focus more on who you connect with as opposed to who appears to be the most "right."

7. You don't feel the need to rush.

You aren't attached to the timeline anymore; you realize that the need to rush into things is usually a product of insecurity and fear rather than passion and love.

8. You believe there is love out there for you.

If you don't think it's there, it won't be. You simply won't open your mind or heart to the friend of a friend you get set up with or the person sitting next to you at the bar. It all begins with how you *think* about your love life, and the most important thing is that you believe you're going to have one.

9. You're choosing to be yourself more than you're trying to be someone else's ideal.

You're at the point where convincing someone that they love you for someone you're not is scarier than being rejected for who you really are.

10. You'd all but given up.

You were just at the point where you thought you'd never find love again, and that you'd have to be alone forever—and you more or less accepted this, to a degree. It's always when we're most inclined to throw our hands up that the thing we've been waiting for walks through the door.

4

What To Look For When You're Ready To Find Love

Kim Quindlen

Find someone who makes you feel happy and excited, even when everything is boring. Someone who brings you a sense of pure joy, contentment, and peace when you're around them, long after the addictive infatuation stage of your relationship is over.

Find someone you can't wait to come home to at night, or to meet up with for dinner, or to willingly hop in a car with for a twelve-hour road trip. Find someone you feel you could talk endlessly with, even though you feel just as comfortable together in a trusted, peaceful, happy silence.

Find someone who can make you laugh and who also knows when you need to be serious. Find someone who will push you to do the things that scare you, even if the thing that scares you is as seemingly simple as opening up to another human being. Find the person who challenges you not because they're trying to change you, but because they know you're not going after what you truly want. Find the person who loves you as you are and yet makes you want to be so much better than the person you are today.

Find the person who introduces you to parts of the world you wouldn't otherwise have discovered. It can be as literal as hopping on a plane and journeying to a country you would never have dared to explore. But it can also mean being with someone who shows you how different the world can be just ten minutes away from where you live. Find someone who reminds you that there is so much that exists outside of you and your bubble, that there are so many people with stories that have yet to be heard, that there are so many ways you can find meaning in your life outside of the things that have brought you no luck thus far.

Find someone who makes you want to *choose* to love them. Sometimes we're conditioned to think that it should be easy, that our hearts will do all the work, that loving them will be simple because aren't we just so lucky to have found it?! But really, love is hard. Love is really, really hard. It is frustrating, it is a leap into the unknown, it comes with the chance that you will leave with your heartbroken. It takes work, it takes difficult choices, it takes the knowledge that sometimes you're going to have to be unselfish. Our guts can clue us in, certainly, to whether or not a person is right for us. But at the end of the day, love is not something that happens to us. It is something we choose. You fall in love with someone because they catch your eye, they fascinate you, they lighten your world, they show you new ways to live. But you stay in love with someone because you choose to—you choose to make the difficult choice, you choose to put the happiness of you as a partnership above the happiness of you as an individual, you choose to give up your pride. Your heart can feel it, can ignite it. But it is up to you to choose it, to make it last.

Find the person you want to be unselfish for. Find the person you want to write a life with. Find the person you want to continue to choose, long after your heart has let you take the reins.

5

The Kind Of Love That's Still Worth Believing In

Charlotte Green

I believe in waking up to a good morning text. Not because you feel like you need to do it or because you saw someone do it in a movie one time, but because the first thing you want to do when you wake up without me is to feel like I'm next to you. I'll write you just before I go to bed—I always get to sleep later—and when I wake up, your response will be there:

"Good morning, beautiful."

I want to hold your hand across the table at dinner without even realizing I'm doing it. I believe in public displays of affection that never feel public, because we don't even notice anyone's around us. Sometimes we'll be that couple on the train who is kissing in the corner, and neither of us will care, because this world could use a little more love. Some people will look at us and think "Get a room," and we'll wish we could say back, "The world is our room."

I believe in talks, the healthy kind that take on a life of their own and sometimes pass through flushes of disagreement or debate, but always end up back where we should be: the truth.

I'll tell you about my day and not the superficial details that we tell someone who asked "How was your day?" without really caring. I'll tell you about the great things I thought and the sad person I saw in the restaurant, and the way I felt walking across the bridge. Then I'll listen to you talk about your day and wish I could have been there with you.

Because it's about sharing, isn't it? Getting the privilege of sharing someone's life, of being a part of all the things they dream about and achieve and getting to hold them through their failures. Life will fail us, but it will fail us together, and we'll share both the pain and the joy. I believe that it is a great honor to share someone's details, and I will do my best to be your teammate.

Sometimes we'll be friends, though, because I believe that friendships make the best romances. We'll order a large pizza and watch dumb TV shows in our pajamas and get into play fights that turn into something different, something much better. We'll fall asleep all over the house because sometimes we're having too much fun to ever really go to bed. Together, we'll get to be the rowdy kids who want to stay up past their bedtimes and eat junk food while telling scary stories. We'll never feel like we have to grow up.

I believe in you even if I haven't met you, even if I never will. I believe that you're out there—the person who will send me a text in the morning, share the last slice, and be my teammate. Somewhere, you're out there taking your time and waiting for something meaningful to come into your life. And maybe we will never find that perfect thing, and maybe we'll never meet, but that's okay. Because I want to spend my whole life believing in something truly great—something truly spectacular and rare—even if I'm alone in my faith.

6

This Is Falling In Love With The Possibility Of Someone

Alexandria Brown

You let out a breath of air as you look up at your ceiling. Every time you close your eyes, you see their face. And it's not irritating. It's just captivating. So captivating it's keeping you up at night. But why are they even in your brain? It's not like you like them. You promised yourself after the last time that no one was going to break down the extremely high walls you've built around your heart.

But you can't get their stupid face out of your mind. So you're awake. Their face isn't actually even dumb at all. It's beautiful. It's so beautiful that you wonder what it would be like to trace your pointer finger from their forehead down to their perfectly shaped lips. They're also not only physically beautiful; they're that truly beautiful that scares you. They're smart. They're passionate. They're funny.

They're everything interesting that makes you wonder how people like them exist.

And they do exist. They're not the figment of your imagination that you've dreamt of. They're real-life breathing humans that make you want to dive in again. That makes you forget that for a split second that your ex ever existed.

Then you let your mind start to drift to what they're doing right now in this very instant; that maybe right now across town they're awake thinking of you too. That maybe, *just maybe*, this time you're not just dreaming about your future. **Maybe they are your future.**

Then the negativity sets in. What if they're not sleeping by themselves right now? Just because there's a side in your bed that's empty doesn't mean that the object of your affection is also alone. That's what you're thinking, isn't it? You think that the powerful feeling you felt when your hands brushed was only one-sided and that you're crazy. You're insane enough to believe that this beautiful person could ever feel the same way about you.

You're alone for a lot of reasons, remember? You wanted that empty side of the bed next to you because it was once filled with all of your hopes and dreams but now, now it was just empty disappointment. Because you did love before. You loved so hard and so deeply but it wasn't enough. Now here you are, awake, thinking about letting yourself be that vulnerable again. You're thinking about placing your battered and bruised heart into the hands of another person who could just crush you.

You once weren't afraid of love. You weren't so crippled by the thought of letting someone new take your hand and lead you down a new path of love but you are now. Because every trip you've taken has ended with nothing but heartache, and there was no way you were going to let yourself go there again. No matter how beautiful the next person is.

But they are beautiful. And then your mouth twitches for a second before you let yourself smile thinking about the crinkles by their eyes when their face lights up. You let out a small chuckle when you remember how much you laughed at that Internet puppy meme together. Your heart stings a bit when you think about how they talked about their own heartache.

It reminds you that no one is exempt from experiencing heartbreak.

It reminds you that even though they're amazing in every way; what you look like, what you've been through and who you are doesn't determine your ability to be loved.

Your fingers start to burn. You just want to text them and see if they're still up. If they have that one thing to say to you that will ease your mind and give you hope that your feelings are matched. All you really want to text them is *give me love please.*

Lying in your room, looking up at your ceiling, you take a deep breath and let it out. In that moment you make yourself a promise. Love will come and go but if it does go, it wasn't because you weren't enough. It was because life has a way of teaching us lessons that we need in order to get where we're going.

Then your mind drifts back to that beautiful person entrancing your mind, keeping you from sleep and you smile. You smile because this person reminds you of possibilities and that life is full of them. That feeling you feel right now is *hope*. And that in itself is a beautiful thing.

7

Ladies, There's A Difference Between Guys Liking You And Valuing You

Becca Martin

There is absolutely a difference between liking someone and valuing them. Sometimes I think we get more concerned with the fact that someone *likes* us that we forget how important it is to be *valued*. Being liked is good but being valued is so much better.

I like my phone, it occupies me when I'm bored, I can use it as a distraction and it normally does what I say, but I wouldn't say I necessarily value it. I drop it, I break it and as soon as it's broken I start asking my friends if they have old phones I could replace mine with. It's just a phone; it's great when it's working the way I want, but once it stops and starts having problems I look to replace it or upgrade to something new and better.

That is the difference between liking and valuing, and that difference is major.

Don't be with someone because they string pretty little words together that make you feel special if their actions don't match up.

Don't just stand around on the side waiting for a guy because he tells you he like you but follows that line with an excuse about how he isn't ready yet for anything.

Don't waste precious days of your life trying to capture his attention, because honestly, you don't want to be hung up on a guy who keeps you hanging around because he might like you. You don't deserve someone who just likes you; you deserve someone who values you.

You deserve someone who knows just how important you are and how much you're worth. You should be the highlight of someone's life; someone's better half, the part of them that makes them want to be better. You should be that person to someone because a person's values are usually one of the most important things to them.

You deserve to not be taken for granted.

To be valued means that you are appreciated for your role in his life. It means that he respects you and how you feel. It means he doesn't belittle you; he doesn't make your accomplishments seem small and **he doesn't kick you to the curb when something better comes along.** He truly cares about you because he cares about your values and beliefs.

Your values should be everything to you and more important than a guy liking you.

You can claim to be strong in your values, but it's important to realize the company you keep says a lot about how you value yourself.

By hanging around someone who doesn't value you, it's showing others you don't value yourself as much as you should.

Because if you're hanging out with someone who doesn't value you, it's changing your values, not theirs.

If you live your life with the values of trust, respect, and love, you shouldn't settle for someone who doesn't fully invest in you and your relationship. You shouldn't be with someone who doesn't fully trust, respect, or love you just because you're scared to let him go in hopes he might change. All that is doing is compromising your values and internally diminishing your self-worth.

You can't constantly wonder what you're doing wrong, why he isn't as invested in you as you are him when you've let your values down in order to let him in. You want to be the change; you hope you can be the change in him, but love is not meant to change a person into who you want them to be. Love can't change your partner and make them into someone they're not.

You have to know your value in order to be treated right.

A man can like you, but that doesn't mean he will show you the respect you need and deserve. Sometimes you just need to start from where you are with some self-love and care; you need to invest in yourself with a little maintenance, then you will start to see your value build back up again over time. Then you will see how important you are.

Know your worth and practice your values before someone else can come in and start compromising them.

8

Just So You Know, You Don't Have To Be Completely Whole To Fall In Love

Marisa Donnelly

I'm a hopeless romantic. There, I said it.

I love the idea of falling in love, I love the feeling when you start to slip from casual into head-over-heels serious, and I love seeing people that are so dizzy in love with each other they lose all sense of time and place.

I think falling in love with someone is one of the most beautiful things in the world. It's what makes us human—the ability to *feel* and feel such powerful emotion for another person. A smile stretches across my face subconsciously even thinking about it.

But what I find disheartening about today's world is all the rules placed on love. How old you're supposed to be, what it's supposed to look like, how you're supposed to find it or let it find you.

Or the most frustrating: *The person you should be before you fall in love.*

The world gives us so many guidelines, so many restrictions, so many expectations. It puts our feelings into little boxes labeled, 'This Is What It Should Look Like' and 'How To' and I'm sick of it.

I don't agree that there's a specific time when you're supposed to find love. That you can ever be 'too young,' or 'too old,' or too 'childish' or 'not whole enough.'

I get that some people don't *want* to find love at certain times in their life—perhaps because of dreams, or a well-deserved bout of selfishness, or a longing to pursue other things—all of this is understandable.

But you don't have to have it all figured out just to fall in love.

You don't have to know exactly who you are before you can love another person.

I've read so many things about 'finding yourself first' or 'loving yourself first.' I get it, I really do. It's important, if not essential, to find your self-worth in *yourself* rather than another person, **but you don't have to have your entire sense of self understood before you get into a relationship.**

You don't have to feel like you need to fix all the pieces of yourself before you fall in love with another person. Sure, you don't want to be damaged goods, walking around in pain and self-pity. **But you are still lovable in all your forms and in all your stages.**

And there are going to be plenty of things you won't quite know about yourself before you date. *That's what dating and falling in love are all about—discovering who you are and who you are with another person.*

There's no such thing as knowing exactly who you are, and no such thing as being completely perfect before loving someone else.

You are continually shifting and growing and changing. You will continue to go through trials and triumphs. What you want won't always stay the same, and what hurts you will continue to shape you, even when you're knees-deep in love.

There's no way to know exactly who you are, to love exactly who you are before getting into a relationship because you're not just a one-dimensional being.

Sure, you want to have a sense of your desires and purpose before jumping into something serious, but you don't have to, and can't, have your entire life figured out.

The world tells us that you have to be whole before you find someone, that you can't look for your 'other half' because you're already whole on your own.

I get that, and I completely agree that you're whole on your own. But that doesn't mean you push people away because you feel like you're not quite there or you want to discover this 'wholeness' even more.

If you're already whole on your own, then finding who you are is irrelevant.

You're already whole and capable and strong on your own. And falling in love doesn't change that. It just allows you to be whole with another person.

So stop keeping yourself from the beautiful relationships you could be in. Stop trying to find yourself when you've already been found. Instead, try to find even more of yourself in this incredible thing called love.

We're never going to have all the answers, never going to live perfect lives, never going to know exactly what it is we're chasing, or who, exactly, we are. That's why all the rules about love and when and how you should find it are completely stupid.

You find love because you want to find love, because it happens to you out of nowhere, because you pursued it, or because you let it find you right where you are in the moment.

Love isn't about 'How Tos' or guidelines or making sure you've checked everything off on a list before you open up to the idea of it. Love is about letting yourself feel nervous and excited and unsteady and uncertain but then closing your eyes and falling just the same.

It's not about when or how or who you're supposed to be before finding it.

It's about letting it happen, letting yourself feel, letting your fears go.

About being yourself and being with someone who makes you feel not like a complete version of yourself, but an *even more complete version of yourself.*

Because love doesn't define you, it builds you. It doesn't complete you, it compliments you.

You are beautiful on your own, but you shine even brighter in love.

And maybe I'm just a hopeless romantic, but I'll never stop believing its worth it. And I hope you won't either.

9

Look For The One You Want To Spend Every Second With, Not 'The One' You're Fated To Be With

Mélanie Berliet

Maybe you don't believe in Destiny or Fate, but you don't need to. You're too pragmatic and too grounded and too well educated for that. You don't dream of fairytale endings. You watch romantic comedies with one eyebrow raised, understanding that the cheesy moments that tug at your heartstrings and make you cry are unrealistic—corny climactic scenes designed to entertain and to distract you from real life. Even as you weep, overwhelmed with the feels, you don't really believe that those on-screen couples live happily ever after. You see the disagreements, misunderstandings, and temptations peppering their fictional futures.

It's not that you don't believe in romance. It's just that you're too sensible and too experienced to romanticize relationships.

You know better than to latch onto fantasies and false notions about what true love is, or what long-term togetherness actually entails. You understand that maintaining a relationship takes work. That commitment and fidelity aren't magical things that sprout up between lovers when Cupid's arrow strikes. That nurturing loyalty, faith, and trust is tough.

You know that all couples fight. You know that you will not always wake up feeling overwhelmed by affection for your significant other. That a lifelong partnership involves ups and downs and prolonged periods during which you feel neither better nor worse than just okay. You know that couples face doubts, uncertainties, and trying times. That you're bound to ask questions you wish you didn't have to, and wonder whether you've made the right decisions after all. That you'll live and love and make mistakes in the process.

You know there isn't one person out there who's the exact right fit for you, no enchanted glass slipper of a human who will suddenly make your entire existence more spectacular. You don't expect the Universe to go out of its way to unite you with the absolute perfect partner. You know that there are many possibilities out there, in fact. And that every single choice you make day-to-day impacts your specific path, including who you become and who you encounter.

You don't believe in "the one" in a traditional, fatalistic sense. **You believe in *the one* that you get to pick—the one you'll promise forever to and build a life with.**

You're looking for the one you can't stop thinking about right after you meet. The one you want to spend every single second with, knowing that your lustful obsession will eventually transform into a deeper, more satisfying, more powerful connection. The one who makes you smile even when they're not around because the very idea of them delights you. The one who makes you laugh out loud 'til you're rolling on the floor, or peeing in your pants. The one who doesn't care if you snort when you giggle, fart when you sneeze, or drool when you sleep.

You're looking for the one who wants to stay in on a Friday night so you can do nothing but watch movies and eat pizza on the couch. The one who makes you feel beautiful, whether you're wearing a sexy dress or sweatpants and an old T-shirt. The one who genuinely adores your every quirk and flaw because they appreciate you for exactly who you are. The one who urges you to share all your hopes, dreams, and secrets as you lie side by side in bed, forgetting what time it is as you talk late into the night.

You're looking for the one who listens to you without judgment. The one who makes you feel safe just by looking you in the eyes, or holding you tight in their arms. The one you can talk to without actually saying anything out loud. The one who inspires you—who pushes you to think and challenges you unexpectedly. The one who introduces you to new things, and urges you to take risks you wouldn't otherwise embrace.

You know that *this one* will drive you absolutely insane sometimes. That *this one* will fuck up and say hurtful things and make you cry. That *this one* will demand forgiveness and compassion and patience and understanding. You know that *this one* will bring out the worst in you sometimes. That *this one* will test   you   repeatedly   and   that   you'll have to choose them again and again and again over time. That *this one* will be imperfect and that your life together will be imperfect, too.

But you also know that lasting love isn't for the faint of heart, and you're okay with that.

Staying with *this one* won't be easy, but they are THE ONE you're meant to be with.

10

I Fell In Love With You Slowly, And Then All At Once

Bianca Sparacino

When you kissed me you became,
more than just a person.

When you kissed me you became,
the echo of my words,
the tangle in my voice.

You became,
every colour in the sky
on a ripe summer night,
the taste of apricots on my lips.

Suddenly,
without me noticing
you became a living,
breathing,
part of my world.

Suddenly,

without me noticing,
you became a living,
breathing,
part of my soul.

11

I Want Every Day With You To Feel Like The First

Nicole Tarkoff

The beginning phase is always the best, and apparently we're in it, and if what '*they*' say is true this feeling will run out, but I don't want to think about the day when I wake up not feeling the way I do right now with you.

I want every day with you to feel like the first.

I want it to feel like the beginning, because even if we're far from day one we should still remember how to love each other, how to make one another feel special, and wanted.

I don't want the butterflies to be replaced with exhaustion, or annoyance, or spite. I want the butterflies to stay. I still want the same smile to unconsciously appear when I look at my phone and see your name, the smile that happens unintentionally, the smile that happens when everyone around me knows I'm thinking of you.

I still want to feel like I never want you to leave, and I still want to feel an unnecessary loneliness when you do. Because I know I'll be seeing you again soon, but I still want it to feel like it's never soon enough.

I still want there to be effort. I still want the happiness to be maintained, and for each of us to continue to do the little things that show how much we care. I still want to show you that you matter, to show you that even if there's a time in my life when other things come before you, you still have a place here.

I still want the laughter to be exhilarating.

I still want *your* laugh to make *me* laugh, and I still want to think, 'Wow, I love him' when it does.

I still want you to be the first thing I think about when I wake up. I still want *you* to think of *me*.

I still want to unknowingly bring you up in daily conversations, to talk about how wonderful you are without even realizing it.

I still want you to give me a reason to feel lucky, to feel lucky that someone like you would love someone like me. Someone who makes love feel certain, someone who makes *me* feel certain.

I still want that nervousness, the same nervousness I felt when you first whispered that you loved me. When I admitted I was scared, and you reassured me that I didn't have to be.

I want the feeling of beginning to endure until the end.

I want to make you feel like every day with me is the first, and I want to make you feel like you'll never have to worry about there being a last.

12

You Are The Story I Never Want To End

Katie Ray

Three months. 90 days. ¼ of a year. At age 25, this equates to 1/100 of my life. 1%.

It seems negligible, that tiny number. One penny's worth of my days, but it has been worth so much more. I met you three months ago today. It's hard to believe it was so short a time ago because you have already integrated yourself into my life in so many ways. We're at the "official" stage, but we've only just begun. We've bustled, all grins, through the index. Now we're on page one. A fresh new story. I find myself reading every line of you, inhaling your words and your unspoken movements, excited for the volumes to come.

Three months ago, I searched your face, examined your features as you told me about yourself over candlelight—you were a novel I knew nothing about.

I watched your hands underline and emphasize your point, your eyebrows punctuating your stories with excitement and surprise. Our plot lines began to weave together: characters met, adventures were had, conflicts were conquered.

I know that this part—the exposition—brings with it newness and excitement. The anticipation of what's to come. We're still careful, feeling one another out and cautious of "messing up" this budding relationship. It carries a shyness with its fragility: a sneaking-into-the-bathroom-to-brush-your-teeth-at-dawn mindset. Our understanding of one another's character is still developing.

As humans, it is inevitable that past chapters influence our perception of this new thing; they affect the boldness of our font and the transparency of our dialogue. Our wounds and sensitivities are earmarked, worn with constant reference. But with this new introduction, if you're lucky enough, also comes a new tone: a hopeful, bright-eyed one. The crisp pages overrun with words that are full of meaning and actions that are bursting with expression.

Three months into it, I now know what it's like to hold your hand, how you squeeze mine in your sleep. I've memorized the two dots in your right eye that glimmer when you crack an inside joke with me. I feel immediately relaxed when you pull me to you and kiss the top of my head, inaudible, but so powerful.

I feel your fingers on the small of my back as we walk, the electricity running through me to my toes. I can predict the moment right before you reach up to run your fingers through your hair, whether from a falling strand or out of stress. I treasure this time—the attention to little things, the learning, and the thrill of unwritten chapters—and know it won't always be this way, this shiny and new. No matter though. Just like a favorite story, our tale will become one that may be familiar, but its message is transformative. It's one you don't ever want to end.

Fittingly, you've moved into a new apartment, a blank page. I absorb every detail of our time together, especially in this new setting, eager to remember every bit of this part of our story.

Last night I studied the cursive of the cord on the floor, the lamp's light casting long shadows onto the high ceiling. I could smell the scent of the dinner you had cooked, thought about your one-shouldered shrug when I thanked you. "It's nothing special, but I wanted to make it for you," with a sheepish smile.

I felt the newness of your sheets, soft against my cheek, the folds not yet fallen out. Humming, your fan put a chill in the room, but the heat of your legs tangled with my own kept us warm. My eyes traced the baseboards, so clean and spotless. Your furniture, your apartment, us—everything here is so new. No bent corners here; no dust has settled yet. Time will change that, but it just means feeling more like home.

13

I'm Tired Of Playing By The Rules, I Just Want To Love You

Ali Guerra

I'm tired of the dating game.

I'm tired of the incessant desire that humans have to chase the things that they can't have, and then run the other way when they finally catch up.

I'm tired of having to pretend that I am not interested and play the role of the "cool girl" in order to latch your attention from across the room.

I'm tired of the rules when it comes to communication and having to wait 5, 10, or 35 minutes to reply to a message. Setting my clock a minute too fast so that I don't accidentally drunk-text you my feelings before schedule.

I'm tired of taking screenshots of our conversations and e-mailing them to my friends so that they can scrutinize your words and deem you worthy or tell me that you are just a fuckboy.

I'm tired of feeling torn between feeling guilty for sleeping with you on the first date or fearing that lack of a phone call the next day if I don't, or fearing that lack of a phone call the next day if I do.

I want to write you a novel of my feelings for you without worrying about whether or not your "read-receipt" is on, and I want to spit out a mouthful of flowers and poetry on your doorstep when it tells me that you did, in fact, read my message.

I don't want to wait to tell you about the scars on my inner thighs or about the detrimental nightmares I had as a child because when we met you were a blank page I wanted to stain the blood from my hands with.

I don't want to wait to give you my body and my heart and my mind simultaneously, because I am not the misunderstood girl who is afraid to let you in.

Or the cool girl who is too cool to stay or the crazy girl who wants too much too fast—but maybe because I can be all three.

I want to stand in front of you bare-skinned and exposed of all my fears and insecurities and demons and aspirations and desires, and I want you to do the same.

I don't want to follow the rules and miss the day when I could've called you mine because our misguided, passive gestures were miscommunicated.

I want to tell you right now.

14

I Want A Love That Scares Me

Maggie Morgan

A paradigm shift has occurred inside of me within the past few months; a total change of perspective, this uprising has made me wipe away every single thing I have ever thought to be true. At first, it made me mad. I was angry that I had lied to myself for so long, or more so that I had been so naive as to fill myself up with everything everyone told me. I took everything as fact–if you said it with just the right amount of authority, I believed your "it" to be true. I'm not mad any-more, though. I am floating. The me I had held on to for so long, out of fear and out of security, is slowly disassembling and reshaping and becoming something entirely new.

It is because of one thing; a love that is not complacent.

I had become accustomed to a comfortable kind of a love. An intertwined emotional state that wasn't ablaze with passion, but kind of just a placeholder that felt warm enough to keep me safe. This kind of love wasn't bad, it had its own worth and its own place in my life—but it wasn't the kind that you hear about once in a while. It wasn't the kind of love that meant celebrating 50 years together at a state park with all your family and friends, still looking at each other as if you had just met. It wasn't the kind of love that meant feeling his hand on your back, after years of this familiar touch, and still having it send an electricity from the back of your spine to right behind your ears. It wasn't the kind of love that meant catching his eye and feeling your own fill up with tears because you are so goddamn happy he is yours.

It was just there.

I had a lot of these loves. Ones that I thought were "just how it was." You meet someone, spend time with them, learn to put up with their bad habits and terrible missteps and then we call that "love." You move around your insides so theirs can shove in, but it really wasn't a comfortable fit. You learn to apologize for them, to say to yourself "this isn't how it will always be."

I thought that's what love was but the truth is, it was the start of settling.

Not until this love have I been able to recognize that all the others, though they won't ever leave my heart, were really nothing more than lessons. When I first started to experience the distracting, buzzing, nearly heart stopping feeling that I now have every single day—I thought it must be a bad thing. Something that shakes our bones, challenges our beliefs, and something so unfamiliar—how can that be anything but dangerous? **But this uncertainty is what makes it so fucking real.** I want to wake up every day, for as many days as I can think ahead, and I want to feel scared. I want to look at him and not know what he's thinking.

I want to be with him and say nothing at all because the way I want to pour myself into him cannot be said out loud without dulling its meaning. I want to watch him dance badly, get dressed clumsily, laugh too loudly, and sing off key because that is what makes me love so deeply. I am so scared, every day, because with him I have something to lose. All my other lessons, they hurt to say goodbye to but it didn't mean I couldn't fill their place with something else. This love means risking it all and losing this new shade of color that life has suddenly become.

I never want to be comfortable again.

15

There's Something So Right About How Wrong You Are For Me

Kendra Syrdal

You and I are not puzzle pieces.

We do not fit perfectly together to form the corner of a poppy field and sit hand and hand gazing at how symmetrically our fingers meet. We did not find each other and fold into the other's with ease, with grace. We are not completely made up of some sort of imagery that makes people smile and say, "That makes sense."

You and I are vinegar and baking soda. We're pickles and ice cream. We're absolutely no Sonny and Cher. We're the similes and metaphors for things that do not belong together, because darling, we do not make sense.

You and I are, for all intents and purposes, completely and utterly wrong for each other.

You are all stability and "This is what I want." I am always running and jumping and am full of uncertainty. You are more maps, I am more road less traveled. You are alarms being set and I am staying up until 3. You want a period at the end of a sentence while I'll settle for an ellipsis.

Darling, there's nothing about us that should add up to love so why, *why* am standing here with my heart in my hand so desperately hoping you take it?

You make me so, so mad. The way you march around in those stupid boots, yelling about the government and the things you believe makes me want to scream and shut your mouth forever. You do not listen and love the sound of your own voice more than anything.

You're terrible, *and I'm terribly smitten.*

I am broken and you don't have the patience for putting pieces back together. When I flinch you don't notice, when I retreat you don't come looking, when I say I'm sad you want me to get over it. Logistically, you are not what I need.

So why am I sitting here, trying to read you like a prescription I so terribly hope is going to work because I like the way it tastes?

On paper the idea of you and me is completely ridiculous. We should cut our losses, say "at least we tried" and quit while we're ahead. We should throw up our hands, call it a good game, and go on our merry way.

But here you are, trying to fit into my bed. Here you are, trying to figure out how to take a deep breath and listen. Here you are, asking for glue and instructions to try and mend me. Here you are, giving it a shot.

And here I am, letting you.

Here I am, saying "Go ahead" and reaching out my hand. Here I am, speaking slowly and making my needs known. Here I am, saying "I feel" instead of "You need to." Here I am, waiting for you and being patient.

Here I am, making room.

There are so many reasons why you and I should just not. So many reasons to toss up our hands in defeat and walk in opposite directions. So many excuses we could make about how wrong we are for each other and why it's just a waste of time.

But instead, we're just looking for excuses to come back. Instead, we're still here.

Because maybe wrong is just what we need. Maybe we've been studying ingredient lists for so long we've forgotten what it's like to just crave something and go for it. Maybe we've forgotten that two elements that seem like a bad idea can actually make an explosion like no other. Maybe we forgot that what may seem like two different voices, can actually make some truly incredible harmony.

Maybe wrong is the only thing we've ever gotten right.

Maybe.

16

I Don't Want To Fight For You–I'd Rather Fight With You

Mike Zacchio

Every time the thought tiptoes across my mind an internal debate breaks out—one side defending the point, the other arguing selfishness: I don't want to fight for you, whoever you are or wherever you may be.

I'll fight for you if I have to—in times of sickness, or despair, or injury, or anything else that is out of my hands—but I don't want to fight for you if I don't have to.

I'd rather fight with you.

Contrary to what everyone tells me, I don't think you will miraculously come into my life one day and all will make sense in the world. I don't expect it to be easy, but I also don't plan to unnecessarily bend over backwards for trivial matters.

All relationships are work and all will be stressful at times, but I don't plan to exhaust energy when we're the ones creating the work or the stress. There are certain events that will occur in our life that are beyond our control, and I plan to reserve my time and strength for when we have to face them together.

The loss of a job or a loved one, an unplanned expense—any of these are more than enough of a reason to fight and claw with you to overcome whatever obstacle is in front of us. I will fight with you then, and always, to pass the storm together. I think any successful couple would agree that their spouse would do the same.

But I don't want to fight for you.

I don't want to have to reel you back in because you're drifting away from me and I can't figure out the cause or solution. I don't want to have to prove my love to you because even if you're the most insecure woman in the world, there won't be a doubt in the world that everyone around us will know how much I care for you and that you're the only woman in my life.

Maybe it is selfish, but I at least want the basics to come easily: boy meets girl, girl meets boy; boy likes girl, girl likes boy; boy asks girl out, girls accepts boy's request; boy and girl live happily ever after. I honestly don't think any of those are lofty hopes or expectations.

Is it too much to ask for mutual attraction, and not a, "Yeah, I asked her out for years until she finally gave me a chance," story? Sure, that's poetic, but that's not the fairytale I want.

I don't want to have to "win you over" as if you're a prize; I just want to have you, with no games, strings, or fine print attached.

I would want to tell our kids about how the two of us knew we were a perfect match for one another, not how Daddy wore down Mommy until she eventually gave him a pity date.

Is it too much to ask for mutual desire and intent? I don't want to chase you just because you feel that your worth will depreciate if you don't make it a challenge. We complicate too many things in our life, and I'm just as guilty as anyone, but I don't see what has to be complicated about me wanting you, you wanting me, and both of us being cognizant to acknowledge it.

I don't want to fight for you. I'd much rather fight with you.

17

Wait For The One Who Loves You How You Deserve To Be Loved

Rose Goodman

Love is not always magical. Not always lingering kisses and butterflies in the pit of your stomach. Not always long talks into the early hours of dawn. Not always your eyes dancing across the freckles on their nose and the scar beneath their mouth, or feeling simply entranced by the way they chew the inside of their lip as their mind wanders to faraway places.

Oh how I wish it was.

How I wish every girl would wait for this kind of love, fight for it even. I wish we could all see ourselves the way others do, a single snowflake in a blizzard. A beautiful, unique, irreplaceable collection of cells. A work of art in an ugly, broken world. The light in someone else's darkness.

Because you are, every single one of you.

But too often I see people accepting less than they deserve. I see strong, wonderful, inspiring women giving cheaters, liars, game players and emotional abusers chance after chance after chance. Me being one of them.

We let them break us and then we pick up those shattered pieces of our heart and glue them back together to give them just one more shot, to salvage any redeeming quality we believe they possess.

Because we want to believe, we spend every night going over and over their distant, vague texts and their throwaway comments and we hold on to them. We store them away in a little box and retrieve them when we need justification for trying again.

He's changed. He said he will try harder this time. He said he'll stop texting her. Lies. Lies. Lies. You see, these men, the manipulators, the gorgeous men with their charming smile, they know exactly what to say. They know how to pull you back in when they feel you drifting, even if they don't love you. Even if they're only a little bit interested, they cannot bear the thought that you're not anymore. They want to keep you hanging on to the tiniest bit of hope that one day, they'll love you back, in all of the ways you love them.

In all of the ways you crave to be loved.

But they won't.

And you'll lose yourself. You'll forget who you are. You'll be driven by your need for them. And you'll find yourself doing things you wouldn't usually, just incase it gets their attention.

Maybe you'll dress differently, maybe you'll cut your hair, maybe you have sex with them, but they still won't love you.

Because they can't.

Because they only love themselves, and you are there to serve them and their ego.

But honey, believe me when I tell you, there are wonderful men out there; I've seen them. The kind of men who will value you, whose only concern is your happiness. These men will look at you like you are magical. Like you possess the secrets to the world. They will fall in love with all of the things you hate about yourself and teach you to love them too.

They will run their fingers through your hair when you're drifting off to sleep and kiss your forehead when your eyebrows are pulled together in that way they always do when you're worried or stressed. They will see only goodness in you and never, ever intentionally hurt you.

So, I ask you, please stop chasing after the guy who doesn't reply to your texts. The one who is only ever interested when you're on your knees in front of him. The guy who consistently lies and cheats and then tells you he's changed. Stop trying to find excuses for his behaviour because you're too afraid to admit that he's just a player. A no-good guy.

You deserve better.

And I know you don't want to be alone. I know the thought of loneliness suffocates you, I know it makes you feel hopeless

but being alone is better than being in a false state of happiness.

Take the time to do all of the things he doesn't allow. Drink wine with your girlfriends on a Friday night and buy that dress that's a little bit 'slutty', enjoy having men's eyes on you, because you are free. You are your own person. Visit your favourite coffee shop and read your novel, lose yourself in distant worlds and try new things. Fall in love with yourself. Take all of those things he said and made you feel, and lock them in a hidden part of your mind, they do not matter, not anymore.

You do.

And one day someone will notice that twinkle in your eyes or the tiny freckle above your lip and they'll start to fall. They'll want to protect you and love you and hold you close and whisper,

You are the world.

Because you are.

18

Everything About This Scares Me, But I'm Going To Love You Anyway

Lacey Ramburger

I'm sorry, love.

This might come as a surprise to you. What am I sorry for? If I were to be honest, I've been holding myself back from you. I haven't really given you as much of my love as you deserve, as what I should. I've only been loving you halfway.

But I refuse to love you halfway anymore.

There was a point in time where I was fearless in the way I loved. Full throttle, all in, some might even call it reckless. I didn't portion out my love, but allowed it to overflow and spill wherever it landed. There was a certain beauty in it, and I remember it well. Now, the way I love comes out differently. It's laced with hesitancy and skepticism; a love that says "I want to give you all, I just can't right now." The kind of love that takes two steps on the right direction and 3 steps back.

What should be an incredible dance between the two of us turns into the "Hokey Pokey"—one foot in, one foot out.

And oh darling, you just don't deserve that.

Some people might say that line and follow it up with a "You deserve better, you should find someone else." That's not where I'm going with this, darling.

You do deserve better, and instead of bowing out, I'm stepping up. I'm choosing to love you fully, because you don't deserve to be half-loved. No one does, regardless of if the reasons are selfish or out of fear of being hurt. You don't halfway love me, and I will do the same by not simply giving you a small part or percentage.

I refuse to love you halfway.

The kind of love that says "I love you" but then holds ghosts from my past against you. Saying "He left me, so you might too." Using the mistakes that he made, that I made, and measuring you up to the things you *might* do. I can call it protection, preparation, even caution. I can try to justify it however I want, but at the end of the day it means one thing: I'm not giving you all of me.

I'll be honest, it won't be perfect. I'm human and so are you, so of course things won't always happen the way we plan or expect. Some days my all will only be a little, because my strength will be spent and my mind weary. It won't be much, but I'll love you with with all of it anyway. Other days, I'll be at the top of my game. I'll be confident with a spring in my step, excited about life and where it's taking us.

You'll see all the best parts of me, and I'll love you with all of them.

I know that you're more than aware of my struggles in the past. You know the things I'm scared of and what keeps me up at night. You've held my hand and reassured me that everything is okay and have been persistent when I've pushed you away. **You've loved me fully in every way you've known how, and I'll never be able to thank you enough for that.**

I used to believe that I could only give you a certain amount of love, because giving you too much might mean heartbreak for me. I didn't see how it would be possible to love completely again, especially now that my first instinct is caution and resistance. Now I see that I can still be cautious without holding back. I will still be afraid, and I won't always get things right, but that fear can be faced one step at a time. Love casts out fear, and loving half way just won't do.

If I could go back 1 time and somehow love you first, I would. Life didn't work out that way though. I say that my love has to be different now because of pain, but truthfully it doesn't. I can still love you fully—the difference is I'm a little more scarred now. I'm a little more broken than I used to be. The great thing about being broken is it gives you a chance for your heart to expand, to grow. Eventually I won't be broken anymore, and I hope you're still by my side when that day comes.

But starting today, I choose to love you fully, in all of my brokenness. Because you are worth it. You always have been.

It's about time I start showing you.

19

This Is How I Promise To Take Care Of Your Heart

Lauren Jarvis-Gibson

I realize I don't know you yet. I don't know the one person who I will love for eternity, the one person who I will write vows to, and who I will cherish until our laugh lines are permanent reminders of the life we shared together. **I don't know you yet, but when I meet you, this is how I will take care of your heart.**

I will know that your heart is a sacred organ. It provides your body with the oxygen you need to kiss, to love me, and to need me. I want you to know that my heart is yours to take if yours can't work as hard anymore. And I want you to know that I will do everything in my power to hold your heart in the light when you can't find your flashlight in the dark. And I will kiss your heart over and over so you can feel my love being washed all over you.

You will be my person. And you will make my heart beat faster just by knowing that I found you and you found me.

I promise to make your heart beat faster and to fill your stomach with butterflies even after thirty years of being together.

I promise to clean up all the scars and cuts that other women have put on it. I will bandage up the memories from broken promises and wasted tears. I won't let the broken past that you rarely talk about weigh you down anymore. I will lift all of that weight off of you so you don't have to be haunted anymore. And I promise to love your new heart just as much as the one that was full of ghosts.

I promise to dance with you in our living room, chest to chest, and kiss you softly. And then I will feel your heart race when I chase you to the bedroom and hear it beat boldly. I will make sure to make your heart race with anticipation, lust, and love for all the years of you and me. I promise to keep your heart safe in my arms. And when it is time to check in for the night, I promise to whisper "I love you" while you snore softly next to me.

I promise to be gentle with your heart. Your past left you sensitive and your lungs, weakened by people who ran over your every word. So, I promise to listen to you when you are angry. I promise to shower you with kind words and never make you wish you never had met me.

I will lift you up and hold your hand when you are reaching for nothing but air.

A piece of your heart will always be a part of me. And mine will always be apart of yours.

And the thing about your heart is that it makes me happy. I promise to make yours happy, too. And I promise to never break it.

20

This Is The Kind Of Love You Deserve

Shani Jayawardena

You deserve someone who wants to give you a fucking text back, y'know?

Someone who wants you, only you, and makes you feel wanted.

Someone who can't help but message you first thing in the morning when the sun light is slow-dancing through the curtain and they're barely waking.

Someone who wants to spend their drunken Friday nights with you, but also their lazy lemonade Sundays.

Someone who holds their one-person umbrella right above you when it's bucketing down so that you're sheltered, even if it means they get soaked through.

You deserve someone who thinks of you, often.

Someone who calls you on the phone at the end of a long day because they want to hear the sound of your voice before they drift off into slumber.

Someone who makes plans with you on a Tuesday evening because the weekend is just too far away and who cares if we have to go to work the next day.

Someone who says definitely, not maybe, and follows through.

You deserve to hear a song on the radio that makes you melt on the inside at the mere thought of this someone.

Someone who could watch you sleeping for hours at a time and be perfectly content in the grace and stillness of that moment.

Someone who steals a cheeky kiss when you're mid-sentence and least expecting to find their lips.

Someone who will happily pig out on pizza with you in bed and not judge the sweatpants and top knot look you're sporting.

Someone who is *just that into you.*

You deserve someone who challenges the both of you constantly; someone who makes you strive to be better each day, because they're trying to be better too.

Someone you can count on to stick around when the shit hits the fan, which it *will.*

Someone who chooses to lift you up, always.

You deserve magic, fireworks, and confetti canons exploding in your clear blue skies.

You deserve someone who will always be careful with your heart because they know just how fragile it already was before they held it.

Someone who's heart aches whenever yours does.

Someone who wakes up next to you each day feeling like they've hit the jackpot, over and over again, and thinking *what on earth they did in their past life to be so damn lucky.*

You deserve someone's complete attention.

Someone who looks at you, and I mean really sees you, and all of the beauty you hold.

You deserve to be someone's first choice.

Someone's best friend.

Someone's partner in crime.

Someone's everything.

You deserve to be loved and loved extraordinarily well. And to be told that you are loved every single day.

Beautiful girl, you deserve no less than this kind of love.

Thought Catalog, it's a website.
www.thoughtcatalog.com

Social
facebook.com/thoughtcatalog
twitter.com/thoughtcatalog
tumblr.com/thoughtcatalog
instagram.com/thoughtcatalog

Corporate
www.thought.is

14905001R00051